20 Answers

❧

Islam

Andrew Bieszad

Catholic
Answers
Press

20 Answers: Islam
Andrew Bieszad
© 2015 Catholic Answers

All citations from the Quran from the Yusuf Ali translation.

Published by Catholic Answers, Inc.
2020 Gillespie Way
El Cajon, California 92020
1-888-291-8000 orders
619-387-0042 fax
catholic.com

Printed in the United States of America

978-1-941663-29-5
978-1-941663-30-1 Kindle
978-1-941663-31-8 ePub

Introduction

With more than a billion followers and fourteen centuries of history, Islam is one of the world's great religions. Among all the world's religions, however, no other has posed as great a challenge to the Catholic Faith. Muslims and Christians have attempted to convert and conquer each other since their first encounters more than a millennium ago, and in the present day Islamic militancy presents an ever-growing threat to Christians around the world.

Islam claims to be derived from the same Abrahamic faith tradition as Christianity, but in many ways the two religions are as different, and as incompatible, as oil and water. What are these differences? And how can we articulate them to others?

My goal in writing this book was to give Christians, and Catholics especially, a basic introduction to Islam: its beliefs, its practices, and its unique challenges to the Faith today. It is my hope this booklet will serve as a firm guide in learning more about this fascinating religion, and as a mission-challenge to the Church in the years to come.

1. What is Islam?

Islam is a religion founded in the year 610 by an Arab named Muhammad who lived near what is today Mecca,

Saudi Arabia. The word *Islam* means "submission:"[1] Islam teaches that its beliefs are Allah's (God's) ordained way of existence, to which all creation must submit. The central creed of Islam's believers, called Muslims, can be found in the concise profession of faith known as the *shahada,* which says that there is no God but Allah, and Muhammad is his prophet.

Islam teaches that Allah, who is the supreme, all-powerful, wholly transcendent God, revealed Islam to different peoples throughout human history. However, all those peoples distorted it with human innovations, which led to social deviancy and corruption. This corruption affected Jews, Christians, Hindus, and pagans throughout the world, causing Allah's pure religion to be obscured. Therefore, Allah appointed a man—Muhammad—who, through the angel Gabriel, would reveal Islam in its pure form to all mankind for the last time.

Muslims often say that Islam is made of five *pillars.* These are basic teachings with parallels in many religions: 1) belief in Allah and his revelations, 2) praying five times a day, 3) giving 2.5 percent or more of one's income to Islamic causes, 4) fasting for one month a year during the Islamic calendar, and 5) making a pilgrimage to the city of Mecca to walk around the Ka'ba, a large cube shaped structure venerated as the first temple dedicated to Allah.[2]

Islam's main place of worship is the *mosque,* often identifiable by elaborate domes and long towers called minarets. A strict Muslim aversion to idolatry means that mosques never contain the figurative religious art—images and statues of God, saints, and so on—often found in Christian churches. For the majority of Islam, religious leaders called *imams*[3] direct prayer services in mosques, undertake theological scholarship, and exercise pastoral authority.

Islamic history during Muhammad's lifetime is generally broken into two periods. The first, called the Meccan Period, lasted from 610 to 622 and produced about a quarter of Islamic teachings. During this time, Islam was a religious cult in the city of Mecca led by Mohammad; preached general morality and made vague threats of punishment in the afterlife for disobedience. Many of the Arabs became annoyed by Muhammad's preaching, and in 622 he was expelled from Mecca and at the request of the Jewish community he was received in the city of Yathrib, which Muhammad later renamed Medina.

This year marks both the start of the Islamic calendar and the establishment of Islam as a political entity. In this period, called the Medinan Period, Muhammad implored the Jews to convert to Islam, and when they refused, he almost immediately changed his message and began to preach violence against them and all who opposed him. This continued and increased in severity up until his death in 632.

During this same period, Muhammad assembled a small band of caravan raiders, which eventually grew into a large army that helped him conquer the entire western Arabian coastline. After his death in 632, these armies set out to conquer the world. Between the years of 632 and 732, Muslims overran all the territory from what is today western Pakistan across the Mediterranean to central France, converting or subjugating the Christian peoples they defeated. Were it not for the Frankish king Charles Martel, who after a three-day battle bested the Muslim forces at Poitiers, France, in 732, it is possible that all of Europe would be Muslim today.

By the year 748, this first great Islamic empire, known as the Umayyad Caliphate, had reached the zenith of its power through its conquest of what is today Uzbekistan and parts of western China. The Umayyad's power began to decline shortly thereafter, though, and most of the Islamic world was politically divided into different and competing governments. Since then, there have been a few other notable Muslim powers—particularly the Ottomans, who conquered Constantinople in the fifteenth century and expanded from what is today Turkey through Byzantine Christian lands before being definitively turned back in central Europe in the seventeenth. Today, Islam's largest populations are found in the Middle East, North Africa, Asia Minor, Central and Southeast Asia, and some Balkan countries, but its numbers are growing in Western Europe, Russia, and China.

2. Who was Muhammad?

Muhammad was an Arab and the founder of Islam. The details of his early life remain shrouded in mystery, but according to Islamic lore, he was born in 570 to a rich man from the Quraysh, one of many quasi-nomadic Arabian tribes from the western coast of Arabia by the Red Sea. He never knew his father, his mother died when he was six, and he was raised by his uncle, a caravan driver, with whom Mohammad regularly traveled on trips from their home in Mecca to the Holy Land and Yemen.

Muhammad's life was typical of a merchant of his time. When he was 25, he married a wealthy widow named Khadija bint Khuwaylid, fifteen years his senior, and fathered six children with her. In his late thirties he retired from trading and became interested in religion. Arabia was the designated place of exile for Christian heretics from the Byzantine Empire, and his city, Mecca, had been an outpost along the Silk Road since the second century B.C., so Muhammad likely encountered many different kinds of people from across the known world.

According to Islamic tradition, one day, when Muhammad was forty, he went out to a cave at Mt. Hira, on the outskirts of Mecca, to meditate.[4] While he was meditating, an unknown spiritual being suddenly descended upon him, grabbed him so hard he could barely breathe, lifted him into the air, and demanded that he read a sentence it wrote in the sand. Muhammad, who was terrified during the entire experience, claimed that he could not read. The being squeezed him even harder and again demanded that he read, to which Muhammad gave the same response. Finally, on the third time, Muhammad miraculously was able to read the words that were revealed to him:

> Read in the name of the lord who created you,
> Created you from a clot;
> Read in the name of the lord who created you,
> Who taught man what he knew not[5]

The being disappeared. Muhammad ran home terrified, and for days he refused to tell Khadija the details of what had happened. When he finally recounted the incident, she and her cousin, a man named Waraqa bin Nawfal, told Muhammad that the being was *Namus*, whom they associated with the angel Gabriel.

Muhammad later claimed that in further experiences with this same being, which he now called Gabriel, he was designated the "seal of the prophets," and assured that his revelations would be perfect, complete, and final. These "revelations" to Muhammad came to constitute the *Quran*, Islam's holy book, and Muhammad claimed to receive them until his death in 632.

Islam bestows upon Muhammad the title of *Al-Insan Al-Kamil*—the Perfect Man—because it holds him up as the ideal model of Islamic belief and life. Any answers to Islamic faith and practice can be found in him, and when there is a question about a debated matter, the answer can be found by asking one simple question: What would Muhammad do?

Muhammad was a man of many contradictions, though. According to Islamic sacred scripture and tradition, he was often far from perfect, and can be seen engaging in acts including but not limited to highway robbery, extortion, sexual assault, pedophilia, contract killings, and mass murder.[6] He also claimed to have been harassed by Satan and genies[7] more than once.

Muhammad died in 632. There is a degree of dispute about the particular cause of his death, but the most reliable story from Islamic sources is that he died slowly from poison hidden in a leg of lamb that an elderly Jewish woman gave to him.[8] Despite this undignified end, Muhammad is one of the most important and infamous men who ever lived. His religion became the greatest rival to Christianity the world has ever seen.

3. What is the Quran, and how is it different from the Bible?

The Quran is the sacred scripture of Islam. According to Islam, the Quran is the literal, uncreated and eternal word of Allah, ever existing within Allah's mouth and perfectly communicated to Muhammad. The word *Quran* means "reading" or "recitation," since Muhammad claimed the Quran was channeled to him from Allah and that he was merely a "messenger," not the author. The Quran contains no historical or situational context outside that of Muhammad's life, since it was "transmitted" from 610 to Muhammad's death in 632, and written in an Arabic dialect unique to Muhammad's home on the Red Sea coast of the central-northern Arabian Peninsula. The book is organized into 114 chapters (called *suras*), and it contains all that Muhammad claimed Allah revealed to him through his twenty-two-year-long career.

Christians believe that the Bible is the inspired word of God revealed to man over thousands of years and written down by many different authors in multiple languages and throughout diverse places in southwest Asia, northeast Africa, and southern Europe. It tells the story of God's relationship with humanity, gradually revealing his divine nature and final plan for man's salvation from his sins. The Bible contains books of history, poetry, prophecy, letters, and narrative stories, written by men under God's inspiration (as opposed to being recited word-for-word by God), and inerrantly communicates God's unveiling of himself and his truths to his people in aid of their salvation. The Bible culminates in Jesus, the fulfillment of all the history and prophecy that went before him, in whom all men could now be reconciled with the Father and set firmly upon the road to heaven.

The Quran is to be understood literally as it is presented. Any ambiguities in it, whether real or perceived, are never to be questioned, since to question the Quran would be an act of blasphemy, and under Islamic law, called *sharia*, this can be punishable by death. Any problems arising from the text are resolved by consulting the *hadith*, the works of Islamic sacred tradition, which provide the historical and situational context in which Muhammad conveyed the Quran. The hadith also include the life and example of Muhammad, since his words and deeds are considered the perfect model of Islamic piety.[9]

The Quran contains passages that show evidence of adaptation from the Bible, Talmud (an ancient Jewish book), Gnostic texts, and oral tales present during Muhammad's time.[10] And there's a curious similarity with Christian revelation, contained in the very claims that the Quran makes about itself. As it says, "Indeed, we have made it an Arabic Quran that you might understand. And indeed it is, in the mother of the book with us, exalted and full of wisdom" (43:3–4).

This "mother of the book" is consistently understood as the Quran's heavenly existence as the word of Allah, reflected in every paper copy of it on earth.

If the Quran is indeed the uncreated word of Allah, however, then there was never a time when it did not exist: it must have existed eternally, one in being with Allah but distinguished from him in person. This sounds very similar to the Christian doctrine of the Trinity, in which God's eternal Word (the Son) is eternally present with the Father in the Godhead. Islam, which wholly rejects Trinitarian theology, seems to transfer the eternal Word from the Son who became God incarnate (Jesus)[11] to the eternal Quran that became Muhammad's book (the Quran).[12] This threat to Islam's absolute monotheism—for the Quran can't be eternal without being divine—has been a problem acknowledged by Muslim theologians since Islam's earliest days, but it has never been resolved.

4. What are the "satanic verses?"

The term "satanic verses," which author Salman Rushdie used as the title for his controversial 1988 book, does not belong to him. It was invented by Orientalist W. Montgomery Watt to describe a small but theologically significant event in Muhammad's life—one that provides part of the necessary foundation for understanding Islam.

During Muhammad's early years, he was said to make religious concessions for the pagan peoples in order to attract new converts. In one case, he told members of his tribe, called the Quraysh, that they could worship their old gods alongside Allah. Muhammad claimed that when he made this statement, Satan immediately went into his body and spoke these words through him:

Have you seen the likes of Al-Lat and 'Uzza, and a third, Manat?
These are the high-flying cranes; verily their intercession is approved.[13]

The first line is still recited within the Quran.[14] The second line, however, is not.

According to Islamic sacred tradition, later that day the angel Gabriel asked Muhammad why he allowed Satan to speak through him. Muhammad said that he didn't know, and that he was sorry. Gabriel then told Muhammad that Allah forgave his sin, and subsequently removed—*abrogated*—the latter verse from the Quran:

Never did we send a messenger or a prophet before thee, but, when he framed a desire, Satan threw something into his desire: but Allah will cancel anything that Satan throws in, and Allah will confirm his signs: for Allah is full of knowledge and wisdom.[15]

This is a hugely significant statement. First, because it asserts that part of the Quran that we have today contains the words of Satan in it—in spite of the Quran's claims that it is the uncreated and eternal word of Allah. Second, it introduces the concept of abrogation, or *naskh*, into Islam. Abrogation allowed Muhammad to renounce earlier revelations from Allah in favor of later ones that contradicted them, and today it gives Muslims great leeway in their personal interpretations of the Quran and Islamic sacred tradition—deciding for themselves which truths have been abrogated and which remain in force.

Naskh effectively facilitates another Islamic theological concept, called *taqiyya*, which permits Muslims to lie to non-Muslims about Islam if it is done "in the cause of Allah."[16] This can include everything from small deceptions and misdirections to manifest lies about Islam, what it teaches, and the promises accorded to one who converts. *Taqiyya* works with *naskh* by allowing a Muslim to quote abrogated passages from the Quran, such as some that favor peace and religious tolerance,[17] as if they were still in force, giving a more benevolent impression of Islam than do the more militant passages that later abrogated them.

5. What are other sources of Islamic teaching?

Not unlike Catholicism, which derives its doctrines from two sources—Sacred Scripture and Sacred Tradition—Islam has a holy book and an authoritative tradition.

As we have seen, Islam's scripture is the Quran, which Muslims believe to be literal, uncreated and eternal word of Allah. The works of Islam's sacred tradition are generally known as the *hadith*. Hadith means "report." Islamic sacred tradition was originally passed from person to person via word-of-mouth reports. These reports were compiled, edited, categorized, and organized into substantial books by Muslim intellectuals in the centuries after Muhammad's death. Each hadith has its own chain of narrators, called an *isnad*, and with it a corresponding ranking about the accuracy of the tradition, ranging from indisputably accurate to likely forged.

The hadith are very important to Muslims for two major reasons:

First, they provide context to the Quran. Since the Quran is merely a book of what Muhammad claimed was Allah's divine word channeled through him, there is no context to any of the passages. The hadith add historical and situational information to the Quranic passages, allowing them to be properly interpreted. All of the most respected and widely read Quranic commentators not only reference the hadith, but also provide entire hadith narrations in their commentaries to explain and support their positions based on a historical-critical reference point.

Second, they provide all of the information known about Muhammad, his life and his works. Since Islamic theological teaching is perfected within the life and deeds of Muhammad, to know and follow Muhammad perfectly is to be a perfect Muslim. Muhammad claims that the Quran is not his own teaching, but Allah's. However, since Muhammad is the Perfect Man he knows perfectly how to implement and apply the Quran's teachings to please Allah. It is by reading the Quran in conjunction with the hadith that a Muslim can bring himself, according to Islam, to spiritual perfection in this life and in the afterlife.

There are many collections of hadith. This list is certainly not exhaustive, but the hadith can be generally separated into three major categories:

- The *Sira* (Life of Muhammad): Written by Ibn Ishaq during the late seventh and early eighth centuries, this is the earliest compiled biography of Muhammad known to exist, written entirely in hadith narrations organized from before his birth and until his death. It is also possibly the most important collection of hadith for pious Muslim and interested scholar alike since it deals exclusively with Muhammad's life and works.

- The Hadith Collections: These were compiled by Muslim intellectuals who spent a notable part of their lives traveling around the Middle East and Central Asia visiting with persons who claimed to have a connection to Muhammad or knowledge of early Islam, writing their stories down, and then comparing them with other hadith for accuracy. The hadith collections are organized by topic into large tomes that concern matters from divine revelation down to Muhammad's personal hygiene practices. These collections are also ranked for accuracy by their compilers based upon their assessment of the information contained therein.

There are six major hadith collections. However, the two most famous and highly referenced by Muslims are the *Sahih Al-Bukhari* and the *Sahih Al-Muslim*. The word *sahih* means "pure," and refers to the accuracy of the traditions relayed within the books. Bukhari was a learned Muslim from Uzbekistan who in the late ninth century, compiled the most accurate, lengthy, and famous collection of hadith. Muslim, an Iranian, was likewise learned, and was a contemporary of Bukhari. His collection is somewhat shorter, but no less rich, with accurate, well-documented information about Islamic sacred tradition.

- *Tabaqat* literature: *Tabaqat* means "generations," and it contains information not just about Muhammad's life, but about his followers and their deeds after Muhammad's death. Tabaqat literature is a treasure of information about Islam, because the stories contained within it are, unlike the hadith collections sourced and edited by Muslims for religious exegesis, relatively unedited. As such, there are many interesting stories that give an intimate insight into the life of Muhammad and his followers.

Along with the words of the Quran, the documents of the hadith form the basis of Islamic doctrine. Shia Muslims would add that the imam (a supreme Muslim leader descended from Muhammad) can also be a source of such information, since Allah will grant revelation unto him. However, this is not the standard practice, and it is considered heresy by Muslims who assert that divine revelation was perfected in and ended with Muhammad. Shia also have other hadith collections that they alone use.

6. What is the difference between the Sunni and Shia?

There are many different sects in Islam, as there are in Christianity. But the main dissension, that between Sunni and Shia Muslims, has been a cause of dogmatically instituted sociopolitical conflict almost since Islam's founding.

The Islamic calendar begins with Muhammad's founding a religious-political community in what is today Medina, Saudi Arabia, in 622. He had already been preaching Islam for over a decade, but with little success. It was at Medina that Islam evolved from a benign and obscure cult to a militant and codified religion with a system of social organization and a standing army with devoted followers. Muhammad's followers curried favor with him to determine the future leadership of the Muslim community, and after his death in 632, two major factions developed among them.

One group believed that the leadership of the Muslim community (the *caliphate*) was to be chosen by a simple majority election. This was the view of many of Muhammad's non-familial friends, converts, and confidants, who said they were following the traditions, or *sunna*, of Muhammad. The other group believed that Muhammad's prophethood was generational and continued through the bloodline of his physical descendants, who possessed by virtue of their birth a special relationship with Allah. This was the view of most of Muhammad's family, particularly his cousin Ali and daughter Fatima. Since this group was smaller, it was referred to by the other Muslims as the "faction," or *shia*.

During the first twenty-four years of the Islamic empire, tension existed between these groups. In 656, after the death of Caliph Uthman, Muhammad's cousin Ali was elected to the caliphate. He lasted for four years until he was murdered in 661 by an assassin from a breakaway faction known as the Kharijites. Shortly thereafter, a man named Mu'awiya became caliph. He had converted to Islam for political gain after having been an ardent enemy of Muhammad for many years, and his rise to the caliphate drove the Shia to turn against the majority of the Muslim community. So opened the Shia-Sunni split, after which a series of wars ensued. By 680 the split was finalized.

Sunni and Shia theology differ primarily over the means of communicating and relating with Allah. For the Sunni, who constitute the overwhelming majority (more than 80 percent) of Muslims, divine revelation is sealed with the Quran and the life and deeds of Muhammad, and no other communication with Allah will take place until the end of time. For the Shia, divine revelation includes the Quran and tradition but also Allah's communications to Muhammad's descendants. Thus the Shia believe not only that Allah still speaks to men but also that divine revelation can change.

For this reason, Shia Islam tends to fracture into many different sects: if two imams conflict over a new "revelation," a new sect forms. In the early days of Islam, most of the conflict centered on the question of which imam would be the last one before the end of the world. Some said it would be the fifth, others the seventh, but most agree it would be the twelfth imam. This last group, called *Ithnata-ashariya*, or "Twelvers," is the largest sect. They believe that around the year 873 the last imam, Al-Mahdi, went into hiding—known to Shia as the "lesser occultation." In 941, it is said that he sent a letter to his deputy Abu Hasan

Ali ibn Muhammad as-Samarri, in which he said that he would not appoint a new successor, and that he would go into a longer period of hiding, known as the "greater occultation." It is said that he will return with Jesus at the end of the world to usher in the Islamic apocalypse. There have been many different persons in modern times claiming to be Al-Mahdi. The most famous ones were Muhammad Abdullah of Persia, who founded the Bahai religion, and Mirza Ghulam Ahmad, who founded the Ahmadiyya Islamic sect found in India and in Indian communities around the world.

There are other minority sects and movements within Islam. Many of these derive from mixtures of Islam with Christian teachings. The most famous of these are the Sufi, whose name literally means "wool-ly," since they copied Christian monks in practicing various forms of asceticism, such as wearing the wool garments of monks. There are also smaller Muslim sects that blend aspects of paganism and Christianity into their worship rituals. Two such groups are the Alawites of Syria, who worship Ali as a god, and the Druze, who worship the eleventh-century Egyptian Fatimid Caliph Al-Hakim "the Mad" as a god.

The Sunni-Shia conflict is as much a political as a religious division, extending to the very inception of Islam, and is tied to the unsolvable question about Allah's relationship to and communication with man.

7. Do Muslims worship the same God as Christians?

The name *Allah* comes from a combination of two Arabic words: *Al*, meaning "the," and *Ilah*, meaning "God." When combined together, the two are pronounced *Allah*: "the God." Allah is, grammatically speaking, the Arabic equivalent of the Greek term *ho Theos* found in Christian scriptures, and is translated into English as "God." From a linguistic perspective, then, it is indeed correct to say that Allah means God. Furthermore, it would be absurd to say that Muslims worship a "different God" from Christians if it meant that there were actually two (or more) Gods in the universe. There is only one God, and inasmuch as religions worship God in truth, they're only worshiping him.

The difference between the Christian God and Islam's Allah is not one of language, or a claim that there are multiple Gods, but a difference of how the two religions conceive God's *nature*. And it's a difference that goes beyond Islam's rejection of the Trinity.

In Christianity, God is love (1 John 4:8). This simple dogma is unique to Christianity out of the thousands of religions in existence. This divinely revealed truth teaches us, among many things, that a) God's nature is love, b) God is good, and c) God will never do anything inconsistent with his being, as he cannot sin against himself because God is love itself.

In contrast, neither Islamic scripture nor tradition directly answers the question of what Allah's nature is. When asked about who Allah is, most Muslims will start naming different descriptive attributes. He is "the Merciful," "the Beneficent," "the Just One," among many others. These descriptors, many of which Christians would also apply to God, are all from what Muslims call the Ninety-Nine Names of Allah, a list of terms Muhammad used for Allah in the Quran. (Pious Muslims recite the names repeatedly as a prayer on a series of beads called *subha* beads.) But notice that all the descriptive terms talk about Allah's *attributes* without saying what Allah's *nature* is. The Christian can describe God both in terms of his attributes and his nature because, through Jesus, God has intimately revealed a part of his nature to us; for Muslims, however, Allah has made no such revelation.

Also notice that at times these attributes directly contradict each other:

The *source of safety* vs. the *one who causes harm*
The *giver of life* vs. the *giver of death*
The *loving* vs. the *humiliator*

Observing Allah's attributes in Islamic scripture and tradition, we see that he is not bound to either good or evil in an absolute moral sense, but merely by the choice that his will elects at a particular moment.

Allah's choices, even in matters of faith and morals, change as Allah wills them to change, as Muhammad taught in the Quran:

> None of our revelations do we abrogate or cause to be forgotten, but we substitute something better or similar: Knowest thou not that Allah hath power over all things?[18]
>
> Allah will establish in strength those who believe, with the word that stands firm, in this world and in the hereafter; but Allah will leave, to stray, those who do wrong: Allah doeth what he willeth.[19]

In Christianity, truth is not true because God says it is true, but because God himself is absolute truth. It is the complete opposite with Allah, for whom truth is true because he says it is, and if he says something different, truth changes. Allah's nature, then, is not love, but *the force of will*: to do what he wills, when he wills it, as he wills it, on the basis that he wills it so because he has willed it so. Right and wrong, good and evil, are not reflections of Allah's unchangeable nature, but of Allah's changeable disposition.

This is one reason why, for centuries, Catholics and Orthodox Christians in the Middle East have seldom used the word *Allah* when speaking about God, because although grammatically correct, the word has been associated with a quite different concept of the divine.

Instead, when speaking of God they traditionally have used the word *Rabb*, "Lord," or *Rabbuna*, "Our Lord."

Since the Second Vatican Council (1962–1965), many in the Catholic Church have attempted to focus on similarities between Christianity and Islam in order to facilitate better interfaith relations. To that end, the council documents *Lumen Gentium* and *Nostra Aetate* both included passages emphasizing similarities between Catholic and Islamic theology: for example, that both point to God's oneness, mercy, and judgeship over the world.[20] But in other significant respects, the two religions hold to quite different concepts of who God is and how he acts.

8. What do Muslims believe about Jesus and the Blessed Virgin Mary?

Both Jesus and Mary appear in the Quran. Islam holds that both Jesus and Mary were sinless, and that Mary was conceived without sin.[21] Islam teaches that Jesus was a prophet of Islam who performed many miracles and who brought down the Gospels[22] from heaven to teach to his disciples and the Jews, and that he did not die on the cross but was assumed into heaven[23] (according to Islamic tradition, he had another man crucified in his place).

Jesus is a difficult person for Muslims and Christians to talk about together. Islamic theology is in its most rudimentary form based upon renouncing Jesus' divinity and the Holy Trinity, and it holds that Christians conspired to corrupt the original message of Islam that Jesus brought.[24] Therefore, Islamic theology not only teaches that Islam is correct, but that non-Muslims are engaged in a conspiracy to deceive Muslims into leaving Islam. This in part accounts for the resistance and sometimes hostility toward Christians who attempt to discuss theological matters with Muslims. It is a problem that has plagued Christian missionary work among Muslims since Islam's inception.

Mary is of particular importance within Islam; in fact, she is the only woman in the Quran accorded any major significance. Muhammad's own daughter Fatima has been compared by many Muslims, particularly the Shia, to Mary, and for many she occupies a pre-eminent place of respect.[25] Some Muslims actually refer to Fatima as *Maryam Al-Kubra,* or "the greater Mary" and the Blessed Virgin *Maryam As-Sughra*, or "the lesser Mary."

Islamic belief about Jesus and Mary is an excellent example of Islamic theology's failure to acknowledge the cognitive dissonance within itself. There is no question, according to Islam's own sacred tradition, that Muhammad not only sinned, but that he sinned grievously, repeatedly, and with malicious intentions. Jesus and Mary, on the other hand, are never depicted or described as sinning. However, Islam still teaches that Muhammad is greater than both—because Allah decrees it so.

Despite his positive depiction in the Quran, however, the mere mention of Jesus' name can be repellent to Muslims, who see Christian belief about him as an affront to Allah's sole divinity. This is not this case with Mary, whom Muslims consider to be one of the greatest prophets who ever lived. And just as Mary always points the way to her son, through Mary many Muslims have come to embrace the Catholic Faith. Many Catholic peoples, too, have attributed their victories over invading Islamic armies to her intercession. Many believe that the future conversion of Islam will only be accomplished with a strong Marian emphasis. In the words of Bl. Fulton J. Sheen:

> Missionaries in the future will increasingly see that their apostolate among the Muslims will be successful in the measure that they preach Our Lady of Fatima. Because the Muslims have a devotion to Mary, our missionaries should be satisfied merely to expand and develop that devotion with the full realization that our Blessed Lady will carry the Muslims the rest of the way to her divine son. As those who lose devotion to her lose belief in the divinity of Christ, so those who intensify devotion to her gradually acquire that belief.[26]

9. What is the Islamic view of non-Muslims?

Islam's distinction between Muslims and non-Muslims is significant because it is not merely about theological differences—it strikes to the question of man's dignity and worthiness of life. Islam teaches that all creation is made to submit to Allah's will and is thus Islamic. Of all creation, man is the only creature that has free will to accept or reject Islam, but although he is born a Muslim[27] he is not created in Allah's image and likeness, as Genesis 1:27 says man is created in God's. He is no different from any other created object. Therefore, not only does man have no share in Allah's nature, but his human worth is an extrinsic quality, not something that is innately part of what he is. The Quran attests to this:

> We have indeed created man in the best of molds, then do we abase him to the lowest of the low, except such as believe and do righteous deeds: For they shall have a reward unfailing.[28]

A person's humanity is thus conditional upon and proportionate to *his belief in and practice of Islam*. As Islam vests a man with his humanity, the choice to renounce Islam divests him of it. He is a person in physical form but with a nature no different from that of a beast, and his humanity can only be restored by his conversion to Islam. This is why violence directed against non-Muslims often provokes little to no objection from Muslim scholars or leaders. A non-Muslim or apostate from Islam simply does not possess human dignity. This view is consistently emphasized by Islamic sacred scripture and tradition:

> And well ye knew those amongst you who transgressed in the matter of the Sabbath: We said to them: "Be ye apes, despised and rejected."[29]
>
> Narrated Ikrima: Some unbelievers were brought to Ali and he burnt them. The news of this event reached Ibn 'Abbas who said, "If I had been in his place, I would not have burnt them, as Allah's apostle forbade it, saying, 'Do not punish anybody with Allah's punishment (fire).' I would have killed them according to the statement of Allah's apostle, 'Whoever changed his Islamic religion, then kill him.'"[30]

Some assume that if non-Muslims are not regarded as human, it is required under Islamic law that they be mistreated. This is not true. In the most liberal but still theologically orthodox application of Islamic theology, non-Muslims or Muslim apostates are permitted to live in Islamic societies as long as they accept the rules of those societies and, often times, the additional laws applicable to non-Muslims alone, called *dhimmi* laws.[31] However, even in such a scenario, no protection is afforded to them outside of the will of the greater

Muslim community. Should any Muslim decide to abuse, harass, or even kill a non-Muslim for his refusal to convert to Islam, there would be no sin attached to it under Islamic law. Such an action would be classified as *maqbul* (permissible), and in the words of Muhammad, *La darur, wa la dirar*—"neither harmful, nor causing harm."[32]

The teaching creates equally serious problems *among* Muslims, and it accounts for the perpetual war that has plagued the Muslim world. For if a person's humanity is conditional upon his belief in and practice of Islam, then an especially pious Muslim is not only more human than non-Muslims—he is more human than *other* Muslims. For many Muslims, this justifies the mistreatment of other Muslim sects; if there is a theological difference between two sects, not only are they mutually able to pronounce the other as an infidel, but they can wage *jihad* (holy war) against each other. Even within one sect, this theology justifies the mistreatment of the less pious by the more pious. Historically, this has accounted for the pattern of solidarity among Muslims against non-Muslims followed by immediate dissension thereafter.[33]

10. How did Islam spread?

Islam has almost always spread by violence. The only two countries that became Muslim peaceably were Indonesia and Bangladesh: the former by merchants through trading and the latter through Sufi missionaries. All of the other historical conversions of peoples to Islam have used, at least to a degree, military force. If we look on a map, particularly in the first century of Islamic expansion between 632 and 732, we see Islam spreading by conquering merchant towns along the old Silk Road, which ran from the far East through Persia and Arabia to Europe, explaining in part how Islam was able so quickly to establish an empire that stretched from Portugal to Uzbekistan.

When Islam conquered Christian territories, conversion often did not happen immediately. It could take several centuries, depending on the area. Muslim rulers sometimes tried to speed up the process by promising Christian apostates money, women, and prestigious offices in government. If the conquered people put up a strong resistance, they were more heavily suppressed, and even exterminated. Those who submitted to Islamic law without resistance, on the other hand, were permitted to exist, and in many cases still do. This is why there are still Christians in Egypt today, for example, but not the rest of North Africa. In Tunisia, Libya, and Algeria, Christians resisted for a century until they were defeated, and the survivors were forced to convert to Islam, flee for their lives, become slaves, or die.

Centuries of Christian-Muslim conflict followed Islam's initial conquests. The majority of this fighting saw the Christians on the defense and Muslims on the offense, as Islamic armies conquered the Holy Land, much of the eastern Roman Empire, and most of the Iberian Peninsula, and unceasingly attempted to invade more of Western European soil. The last major battle between Christians and Muslims on European soil was in 1683, with Christian armies repelling Turkish invaders from the gates of Vienna. However, the roots of the conflict have never abated, since they derive from core principles of Islamic theology.

The reason is connected to Islam's conditional view of human dignity. In Islam, as we have seen, human worth is based upon belief in and practice of Islam. This justifies and even gives incentive for the use of violent means in the service of the conversion or subjugation of non-Muslims. The fourteenth-century Muslim scholar Ibn Taymiyya expounded upon this through his discussion of the "two halves" of the world. The first is known as the *Dar al-Islam*, house of Islam, and it comprises all Muslims and areas under Muslim control. The other half is known as the *Dar al-Harb*, house of war, and it comprises all non-Muslims and their properties. The understanding is that the *Dar al-Islam* will assimilate the *Dar al-Harb* by divine decree—not as a matter of if, but when.

11. What is sharia?

Sharia is the practical application of Islamic theology in daily life. *Sharia* means "way," and it indicates the proper form of conduct for people, businesses, and societies in accordance with Islamic law. The word sharia, or sharia law as it is sometimes called, appears frequently in Western media stories about harsh and violent punishments (lashing, stoning, imprisonment) being handed down for seemingly minute transgressions. Such punishments may seem incredible to Westerners, but they reflect in material form the flowering of Islamic theology. Sharia derives from the Quran and the hadith, as well as from theological writings of Islamic scholars who draw upon the Quran and hadith as their primary sources.

There can be a degree of diversity within sharia when it comes to application. To use a popular example, Islam forbids alcohol; however, when formulating sharia law, the most liberal Muslim theologians would say that although alcohol is forbidden for consumption, it's permissible for medical or industrial applications. The most conservative theologians would say that even merely touching alcohol is a grave sin. Both views, though diverse, are permissible within Islam. It is up to the individual believer to discern which one to accept. (The actual enforcement of such laws in a society, however, often is a matter of political will and physical force.)

Or consider the issue of non-Muslims. Islam does not require Muslims to abuse or mistreat non-Muslims; it only establishes the *permissibility* of doing so. Thus, a more liberal Muslim may legitimately say that non-Muslims have the right to live peaceably in a Muslim-majority society and have nearly all the same rights as Muslims. Another Muslim may say with the *same legitimacy* that non-Muslims must convert or die, and then proceed to enforce such command by his own hand. Both views are correct, and all that separates them is the choice of the individual. This is the reason why there have been times when Christians lived well in Islamic societies, only to have an immediate change with a new ruler. It is also the reason why those who do violence in the name of Islam, and those who refrain from it, can both say they are correctly following their religion.

12. I have Muslim friends who are good and peaceful people. Doesn't that prove that Islam is a religion of peace and that Muslim terrorists are disobeying the teachings of Islam?

There are good and peaceful people in every religion, as there are also bad and violent people. This applies to all groups of people—religious or not—throughout all cultures, places, and times. Every one of us is distorted by sin, and in need of the forgiveness and salvation that Christ won for us on the cross. People will be people no matter where they are, for better or worse. However, the way that they behave does not change what they profess to be the divinely revealed truths of their religion.

To give a parallel example: a 2013 study found that only half of American Catholics believe that the Eucharist is truly the body, blood, soul, and divinity of Jesus. This is a major problem, considering that belief in the Eucharist is central to Catholic doctrine. However, the fact that half of Catholics do not believe what the Church teaches about the Eucharist does not mean the Church doesn't teach it.

The same principle applies to Islam. Some Muslims renounce violent Islamic teachings, but their personal feelings cannot change what Islam teaches is divinely revealed dogma. Like Catholic belief in the Eucharist, the violent imperatives of Islam are not the product of a majority vote that is subject to updating over time with changing opinion and practice. They can't be opposed without opposing Islam itself, and they can't be changed without undermining Islam's very foundation.

An excellent example of this is something briefly mentioned earlier. Recall how some early Muslim theologians, who were called Mu'tazilites, observed that the Quran can't be eternal without being divine. On the basis of reason, they said, the Quran must therefore be created, not eternal. The conflict became so serious that the Abbasid Caliph Al-Ma'mun intervened; in 830 he declared Mu'tazilism to be the official theology of Islam and had the prior orthodox view repressed. This was a period in Islamic history known as the *mihna*, or persecution of Islamic orthodoxy. Following a series of intellectual and material wars over the next two decades, Mu'tazilism was defeated and prior orthodoxy was restored. The core problem that the Mu'tazilites raised still has not been answered logically, and it never will be. Islamic orthodoxy as expressed in the Quran—in that case and in the case of Islam's violent teachings—must persist, or else Islam ceases to be.

Likewise, Islamic theology can never formally separate itself from the use of violence in the cause of Islam; to do so would be to deny what it regards as Allah's literal revealed word and the example of Allah's prophet, the Perfect Man. The typical response from Muslim authorities to Islamic terrorism is, therefore, silence. Inasmuch as there are individual Muslims who categorically renounce violence, to the extent they do so they also renounce Muhammad and the Quran.

13. Isn't it unfair to criticize the Quran when the Bible also contains divine sanction of violence?

There is violence in both the Christian Bible and the Muslim Quran. However, that is where the comparison ends.

Jesus, who is Christianity's highest authority and role model, never used or advocated violence for the spread of the gospel. On the contrary, he rebuked those who tried it.[34] This cannot be said about Muhammad—Islam's authority and role model—who used violence to spread Islam and expressly encouraged his followers to do likewise: "I have been commanded to fight against the people until they testify that there is no god but Allah, and believe I am his slave and messenger."[35]

No one questions that both Christians and Muslims have done horrible things. However, when Christians have done them, they were disobeying Jesus' command and example, whereas Muslims can and do legitimately claim they are acting in accordance with Muhammad's command and example.[36]

Claims about biblical violence inevitably refer to the Old Testament, where God sometimes commands Israel to war. In those instances, however, God was employing the Israelites to execute his justice upon particular groups of people for a specific purpose. Indeed, as the Old Testament relates, the Hebrews met the same justice on account of their sins through the Babylonian destruction of Israel in 586 B.C.[37] In any case, no Jew or Christian believes that in these Old Testament examples God was giving open-ended moral commandments for all his people, present and future, to kill and subjugate others.

The same cannot be said about Islam. The Quran, which was communicated solely during Muhammad's lifetime (as opposed to the Old Testament, which was written and compiled over many centuries and through many human authors) says nothing about violence as the just punishment for sinners. Instead it places heavenly beatitude in the acquisition of power, directly reflected in Muhammad's life and deeds. Furthermore, whereas instances of divine sanction of violence in the Old Testament are time- and place-specific, in the Quran that sanction is a command for perpetual war that enjoins all believers:

> Fight those who do not believe in Allah, nor in the latter day, nor do they prohibit what Allah and his apostle have prohibited, nor follow the religion of truth, out of those who have been given the Book, until they pay the tax in acknowledgment of superiority and they are in a state of subjection.[38]

> They desire that you should disbelieve as they have disbelieved, so that you might be alike; therefore take not from among them friends until they fly in Allah's way; but if they turn back, then seize them and kill them wherever you find them, and take not from among them a friend or a helper.[39]

> The punishment of those who wage war against Allah and his apostle and strive to make mischief in the land is only this, that they should be murdered

or crucified or their hands and their feet should be cut off on opposite sides or be exiled; this shall be as a disgrace for them in this world, and in the hereafter they shall have a grievous chastisement.[40]

O Prophet! Urge the believers to war; if there are twenty patient ones of you they shall overcome two hundred, and if there are a hundred of you they shall overcome a thousand of those who disbelieve, because they are a people who do not understand.[41]

Therefore, when ye meet the unbelievers, smite at their necks; at length, when ye have thoroughly subdued them, bind a bond firmly: thereafter either generosity or ransom: Until the war lays down its burdens.[42]

O Prophet! Strive hard against the unbelievers and the hypocrites, and be firm against them. Their abode is hell, an evil refuge.[43]

The violent episodes found in the Old Testament (along with other aspects of life in the Old Covenant) give way to the peace of the New, as Jesus fulfils and perfects all that went before him. The Quran is a complete inversion of this, claiming that the Christian New Testament is a corruption of God's revelation, while sanctioning violence in a way and to a degree not found in the Old Testament.

14. During the Crusades, didn't Christian armies once do the same kinds of things we criticize Muslim terrorists for today?

For hundreds of years during the Middle Ages, Christian armies from Europe did go to war against Muslim forces. And back then, as today, war was a brutally violent affair.

To answer this question, though, it must first be noted that the Crusades were primarily a defensive response to centuries of military incursions by Islamic forces. By the time Pope Urban II called for the Crusades in 1092, Islam had been at war with Christendom for 460 years. During this time, Muslims had destroyed or wholly subjugated almost all Catholic territories in North Africa, the Middle East, Spain, and Central Asia, and forced the surviving communities to live as second-class citizens under Islamic law. They had taken the holy city of Jerusalem along with many other sacred sites. Military assaults and slave raids by the Ottoman Turks continued unabated against the Mediterranean coastline. All of this was in keeping with directives allegedly given by Allah to Muhammad, and with Islamic teaching on the subhuman status of non-Muslims.

The Church understood well all these facts. So did Spanish Catholics, who after the Muslim invasion of Spain in 711 ushered in the *Reconquista*, which would take 781 years to finally drive out the occupiers. So Urban II's call for Christian warriors to go on an "armed pilgrimage" to the Holy Land to aid in the defense of Christians against the Muslims came as no surprise.

There is no question that during the Crusades, particularly those to the Holy Land,[44] there were bad Crusaders. Their deeds have been well known, and equally criticized by the Church. For instance, Pope Eugene III called for the Second Crusade in 1145 following the massacre of the city of Edessa in 1144. However, the Crusade went awry when infighting among the leaders resulted in the failed siege of Damascus in 1148. Eugene's friend St. Bernard of Clairvaux rightly said that the failure of the Crusade was due to the Crusaders' sins. Likewise, the infamous massacre of Hattin in 1187, where most of the Crusader army was butchered, was the result of the failed attempts at vainglory by Crusader leader Raymond of Chatillon. Then there was the infamous Fourth Crusade in 1204, in which Venetian merchants manipulated the leaders to attack the Christian city of Constantinople instead of Muslim possessions. In addition, historians have recorded cases of Crusaders robbing and pillaging Jews, and even fellow Christians.

However, the great majority of those who went on Crusade did so with good intentions and behaved admirably. Their memory cannot be sullied on account of a few evil men. Consider that most Crusaders went along in order to perform the pilgrimage to Jerusalem, after which they went home. Few stayed behind, and those who did often belonged to one of the Catholic military orders such as the Knights Templar or the Knights Hospitaller. The Crusaders who did stay in the Holy Land earned a reputation for being just, fair, and magnanimous to all, Muslim and Christian alike, and oftentimes ensured the equal treatment of persons from both religions so well that the Muslims came to enjoy living under the Crusaders better than under fellow Muslims. The Muslim chronicler Ibn Jubayr records one such example:

> We moved from Tibnin—may Allah destroy it—at daybreak on Monday. Our way lay through continuous farms and ordered settlements, whose inhabitants were all Muslims, living comfortably with the Franks. Allah protect us from such temptation. They surrender half their crops to the Franks at harvest time, and pay as well a poll-tax of one dinar and five qirat for each person. Other than that, they are not interfered with, save for a light tax on the fruits of trees. Their houses and all their effects are left to their full possession. All the coastal cities occupied by the Franks are managed in this fashion, their rural districts, the villages and farms, belonging to the Muslims. But their hearts have been seduced, for they observe how unlike them in ease and comfort are their brethren in the Muslim regions under their Muslim governors. . . .

The Muslim community bewails the injustice of a landlord of its own faith, and applauds the conduct of its opponent and enemy, the Frankish landlord, and is accustomed to justice from him.[45]

Most of the violence employed during the Crusades had a directed military purpose and end. When there was indiscriminate violence, the Church criticized its own people publicly and even apologized. Moreover, that indiscriminate violence pales in comparison to the wholesale slaughter that Islam has frequently inflicted upon Christians, not with remorse but rather defiant justification. Consider the genocide of Armenian Christians in Turkey (1915-1918), committed with the intention of fulfilling Islamic teachings about non-Muslims, and completely aggressive in nature. Over a million people were murdered or forced to convert to Islam, and an entire culture was destroyed. Yet Turkey still refuses to acknowledge the massacre ever happened, let alone apologize for it.

In history there has been violence associated with all cultures and all religions. However, violence in Christian history is always situational, limited by time, place, and disposition of the involved persons. In Islam, the violence in an intrinsic part of the theology that follows it wherever it goes, and is the natural product of Muhammad's life and teachings as the perfect model of Islamic practice.

15. Is modern Islamic hostility towards the West a result of Muslim memory of the Crusades?

Far from being ever-present in the Muslim mind, the Crusades were often little more than a footnote in Islamic history until the early twentieth century. This is because, from the Islamic perspective, the Holy Land was brought into the *Dar al-Islam* with the conquest of Jerusalem in 637. It was briefly under the control of the Crusaders from 1099 until 1291, after which it was returned to Muslim hands and remained so until the creation of Israel in 1947. Muslims did not bother to ask why the Holy Land was briefly in the power of "infidels," because for them, it is of no significance, and could have been a part of Allah's will. In any case, what mattered for them was that Islam ultimately reigned victorious even if there was a brief interregnum.

The proof of this is found in Islamic writings. There are very few Muslim records of the Crusades, compared with other episodes of Islamic history or especially, Catholic accounts of the Crusades. The first Muslim history of the Crusades was not even written until 1899, under the title *The Wars of the Cross*. This is because, for the Muslim, the historical events are not as important as the idea that the domain of Islam remained intact.

What has proved to be a greater problem for Islamic theologians are countries that once were under the rule of Islam and are now firmly under "infidel" rule.

Spain is a clear example. Muslim armies under Tariq Ibn Ziyad crossed the Strait of Gibraltar in 711 and by 718 had conquered all of Spain, save the northernmost mountain regions, and were crossing over the Pyrenees into France. Spain would remain under Muslim control, at least in part, until Queen Isabella and King Ferdinand conquered the Muslim Emirate at Granada in 1492. Even after this, Spain had to contend with rebellions within its own borders by Muslims pretending to be Catholics until their final expulsion in 1609. After Islam's political (and, gradually, social) influence was expunged, Spain then helped spread Catholicism throughout the world. Seeing the "Jewel of the Muslim West" so decisively delivered to Christians is a challenge to Muslims' faith.

Modern Muslim preoccupation with Israel can be understood in a similar context. Islamic hostility toward Judaism goes back to Muhammad's migration to the city of Yathrib in 622. When the Jews there rejected Muhammad's religion, Muhammad grew angry against them, and over the next ten years he waged a series of caravan raids and tribal wars that not only purged all Jews from Yathrib, but from most of the surrounding towns. Since the initial Islamic conquest of the Middle East, with a brief exception during the Crusades, the land that constitutes the modern state of Israel remained in Muslim temporal control until the mid-twentieth century. With the establishment of the state of Israel in 1948 (whether one argues it is a "Jewish" state or merely a secular state with Jewish roots), that land left the *Dar al-Islam* and re-entered the *Dar al-Harb*, creating for Muslims an intolerable theological quandary.

There has always been Islamic hostility towards Judaism and the Christian West, and there always will be until both have been converted to or subjugated by Islam. Blaming the Crusades from 900 years ago for current-day hostility is unsupported by history, and ignores the more obvious reasons rooted in Islam itself.

16. Doesn't Islam have a special relationship with Christianity and Judaism, because all three religions come from Abraham?

It is true that Christianity, Judaism, and Islam all claim a common connection to Abraham. (The Vatican II document *Nostra Aetate* describes how Islam "takes pleasure in linking itself" with Abraham.[46]) However, as with many other seeming similarities this connection is superficial. When we examine it in more depth, it does not reveal a special relationship between three "Abrahamic religions" but only a clearer contrast.

The book of Genesis (chs. 16 and 17) tells the story of Ishmael, Abraham's eldest son born illegitimately from his slave Hagar because Abraham did not believe that God would provide a descendant from his wife,

Sarah. After Sarah later conceived and bore Isaac, she prevailed upon Abraham to send Hagar and Ishmael away into the wilderness. The understanding among Semitic people is that Isaac became the father of the Hebrews, while Ishmael became the father of all the other peoples in the region. This included those in Scripture who were belligerent toward the Hebrews, such as the Amalekites, Edomites, and the Jebusites, but also the Arabs. Scripture tells us that an angel appeared to Hagar and said of Ishmael, "He shall be a wild ass of a man, his hand against every man's hand, and every man's hand against him; and he shall dwell over against all his kinsmen."[47]

Before his martyrdom in India, the apostle Thomas—the one who did not initially believe Jesus' resurrection—evangelized the Arab peoples in what is today Jordan, eastern Syria, and northern Iraq; and for six centuries after, the Faith had a notable presence among certain segments of the Arab population. The middle part of the Arabian Peninsula, where Muhammad was born, raised, and first began preaching, remained a stronghold of paganism as well as of Christian heresies, but Arab Christianity's roots nonetheless go back to the time of the apostles.

Christians believe that God revealed himself to Abraham, and because of his obedience God promised to make his descendants as countless as the stars.[48] Genesis tells us that Abraham's blessing passed to his son, Isaac, and then to his grandson, Jacob. Through this physical line, the twelve tribes that constitute the Hebrew people came into being, and from the tribe of Judah came Jesus. Christianity and Judaism are truly "Abrahamic" religions in the sense that they accept the same revelation about Abraham's life and deeds, and profess the same beliefs about Abraham's blessing and its subsequent effects (except that the Jews do not acknowledge Jesus as the Messiah). As Jesus said, "[S]alvation is from the Jews."[49]

Islam likewise holds that salvation began with Abraham, but that is the only similarity. For the Quran claims that God's blessing passed to *Ishmael*,[50] not Isaac, and that it was Ishmael whom God told Abraham to sacrifice, not Isaac (see Gen. 22:2–8). The great irony about this insistence is that Islam also holds that all of the other prophets and messengers who came from the Jews descended through *Isaac*. Islam teaches that all the persons in the Bible about whom the Quran also speaks favorably, such as Moses, David, and Jesus, are descended from the Hebrews and later, the tribe of Judah. Only Muhammad, the "seal of the prophets," is descended from Ishmael. Islam offers no explanation for this inconsistency other than that it was Allah's will.

Another reason, though, may be that it was necessary to give Muhammad a justification for his claims to prophethood. As we saw earlier, Arabia was a place of exile for Byzantine heretics. Islamic sacred tradition says that Muhammad knew and conversed with Christians as well as Jews, and was familiar with Christian and Jewish teachings. He knew that he was an Arab and not a Hebrew, and that he didn't have any particular characteristics that would designate him as a prophet. It would have been very hard for Muhammad to claim to be a prophet with a message that replaced Christianity and Judaism. But if Ishmael's line was the blessed one, Muhammad could claim to be the great prophet from the Arabs.

Accordingly, Muslim scholars have attempted to construct elaborate genealogies in order to prove Muhammad's connection to Ishmael. If he were not related to Ishmael, not only would he lack God's blessing and therefore not be a prophet, but the law he gave in the Quran would be false.

One of the other key components of Muhammad's connection to Ishmael is in the fulfillment and execution of the Mosaic Law. Islam holds that Moses received the law and gave it to the Jewish people, but they corrupted it out of malice just as the Christians corrupted the gospel given by Jesus:[51]

Ibn Abbas said, "Why do you ask the people of the scripture about anything while your book [Quran] which has been revealed to Allah's apostle is newer and the latest? You read it pure, undistorted, and unchanged, and Allah has told you that the people of the scripture [Jews and Christians] changed their scripture and distorted it, and wrote the scripture with their own hands and said, 'It is from Allah,' to sell it for a little gain. Does not the knowledge which has come to you prevent you from asking them about anything? No, by Allah, we have never seen any man from them asking you regarding what has been revealed to you!"[52]

Muhammad claimed that, as Allah's chosen prophet through Ishmael, he was the one to correct and seal for all eternity Allah's law: through the preaching of the Quran, the example of his life, and the practical application of the law, sharia.

In sharia we see Islam's stark contrast with Christianity. The law written on the heart by grace[53] is uprooted and replaced with a law written in a book—a book that contradicts and cancels itself as Allah wills. The easy yoke and light burden[54] promised by Christ to his followers with the promise of the beatific vision is abandoned in favor of a law that gives license to carnality and worldliness so long as the believer follows a myriad of complex and inconsistent regulations.

Islam claims that its theology and practice, as articulated through the words and deeds of Muhammad, is the purest form of the religion Abraham practiced. Christianity holds that God's revelation to man began with Abraham and was fulfilled in

Christ. For the Muslim, the fulfillment of Islam is believing in and practicing what Abraham did—according to Muhammad's version. For the Christian, Abraham was a precursor to a greater and eternal fulfillment of God's revelation: the gospel, and the salvation that Christ promised to those who love him.

17. Aren't Muslims pro-life, and our allies in the fight against secularism?

Some Christians look to Islam and see potential partners in their advocacy for the unborn, for traditional marriage, and generally for the rights of people of faith in an increasingly secular world. And it's true that some aspects of Islamic morality and practice seem to mirror Christian belief. But upon deeper investigation, the similarities prove to be unreliable.

Islam is not pro-life in the way Christians understand the term. As we have noted, to Muslims the value of human life is conditional upon sustained belief in and practice of Islam. A non-Muslim has no human dignity, and Muslims whose practice is considered less pious or correct have less dignity than more faithful practitioners.

The general agreement throughout Islamic history is that abortion is to be forbidden. However, all major Muslim schools of thought also agree that the soul does not enter into an unborn child until the fourth month. Therefore, it is permissible to abort up to that time.[55] (Some Muslims consider themselves pro-life in the Catholic sense of opposing all abortion, but this is a uniquely modern view.) The legal status of abortion in Muslim nations varies, but in many places it is still permitted in some circumstances under the guidance of Islamic teachings. Compared with Christians, among Muslims there is very little debate or activism over abortion. Islam is much more concerned with obedience to Allah's dictates in the Quran.

Some point to Muslim nations' sympathy with the Vatican and pro-life groups at United Nations conferences on family and life issues—such as those in Beijing and Cairo in the 1990s—but such cooperation has sharp limits when it comes to abortion. Indeed, at Cairo in 1994, Muslim participants turned down the Vatican's appeal for help in removing language referring to abortion as a woman's right, and such language remained in the final conference documents.[56]

Muslim countries have not legalized same-sex marriage, as some Western countries have done. But that does not mean that Islam has a view of marriage similar to that of Christianity. In Islam, marriage is essentially a sex contract for generating legitimate children. It is not a permanent, loving, exclusive union as in the orthodox Christian ideal; in fact, according to the Quran it can be dissolved at any time by the husband if he pronounces the word "divorce" three times in front of his wife. (A woman can theoretically divorce her husband in Islam, but it is very difficult to do so.) If there are any contested issues in the divorce, a Muslim man only needs the testimony of four Muslim male witnesses, and all his wife's testimony (regardless of the number of witnesses she brings) is rendered invalid.[57] The Quran permits a Muslim man to have up to four wives through whom he can produce legitimate children.[58] In addition to these wives, Islam permits a man to have an unlimited number of sex slaves.[59]

Not all of these Islamic teachings about marriage are perfectly reflected in all Muslim nations' civil laws. As with even the most uniform societies, no two are always alike and there will always be differences in practice. However, the theological bases upon which these beliefs are founded in Islam are never questioned.

Islam's teaching regarding marriage is so radically different from traditional Christianity's, and so anti-woman in practice, that it's difficult to envision a profitable partnership in that area. Real cooperation can only proceed from shared principles.

As far as an alliance against secularism goes, Islam sees itself the ally of nobody but itself, as the Quran clearly states:

Let not the believers take for friends or helpers unbelievers rather than believers: if any do that, in nothing will there be help from Allah: except by way of precaution, that ye may guard yourselves from them.[60]

O you who believe! Do not take the Jews and the Christians for friends; they are friends of each other; and whoever amongst you takes them for a friend, then surely he is one of them; surely Allah does not guide the unjust people."[61]

Some Muslim leaders may seek out "dialogue" with non-Muslims, but this doesn't mean they desire—or see within Islam any conception of—an equal partnership with other theists against a common secular enemy. It doesn't matter that Muslims are monotheists and claim a shared root in Abraham; the idea that Muslims and non-Muslims could work together towards a goal that does not directly promote the advancement of Islamic hegemony (both temporal and spiritual) is non-existent in Islam.

This harkens back to the concept of the "house of Islam" versus the "house of war." Islam teaches that the former will overcome the latter by Allah's divine decree, with the only variables being when Allah wills this to happen and the obedience of the Muslims in fulfilling Allah's will. All that Islam teaches and commands its followers to do is directed to this end of temporal and spiritual domination, and by any means possible, since anything is permissible if it is done "in the cause of Allah."

One historical example to illustrate this: after the re-conquest of Spain from the Muslims in 1492, King Ferdinand and Queen Isabella permitted Muslims to live within Spain. However, they rescinded this order in 1500 because the *mudéjars*, or Muslims living in Spain after the end of the occupation, were fomenting rebellions against the Church and crown. And so if they wanted to stay in Spain, Muslims would have to convert to Catholicism. The Church saw a massive influx of converts, but most of these people converted nominally and not only continued to practice Islam, but continued to foment rebellions. There was even a *fatwa* (religious edict) put out in 1504 permitting Muslims to falsely convert and profess the Catholic Faith so long as they worked in secret against the Church.

Catholic leaders in Spain spent the next century working aggressively among the *moriscos*, or Muslim converts to the Faith and their descendants, to truly come into the Church. One of the most famous of these leaders was St. Juan de Ribera, archbishop of Valencia. After many years of continual rebellions from the Muslim community, even he said that the *moriscos* posed an existential threat to Spain and needed to be removed. He advocated for and eventually realized what became the expulsion of the *moriscos* in 1609.[62]

The issue, then, is not whether Christians should *want* to forge alliances with Muslims on this or that matter. In principle, joining forces with other like-minded religious groups could be valuable in the global struggle against anti-theism and the Culture of Death. The problem is that Islam's own teachings prevent such alliances from bearing much fruit. Whether it is about abortion, marriage, or secularism, the only opinion that is ultimately acceptable is that which consents to and promotes Islam. In the words of the famous Spanish Muslim historiographer Ibn Khaldun when writing about the differences between Christianity and Islam:

> We do not think that we should blacken the pages of this book with discussion of [the Christians' and Jews'] dogmas of unbelief. In general, they are well known. All of them are unbelief. This is clearly stated in the noble Quran. To discuss or argue those things with them is not for us. It is for them to choose between conversion to Islam, payment of the poll tax, or death.[63]

18. Is Islam a threat to the Church?

Islam is the longest-standing temporal threat to the Church, remaining so unabated throughout its fourteen centuries. As in its earliest years, today Islam is growing: making converts, expanding its territory, multiplying its numbers in Christian lands. The threat it poses to the Church is both spiritual and material.

Islam draws its power from its theology. St. John of Damascus (676–749) and Bl. Peter the Venerable of Montboissier (1092–1156), the former once employed by the Umayyad Caliphate and the latter being the founder of Islamic studies in the West, both said that Islam was the culmination of all Christian heresies. It insinuates itself into Christianity's teachings, people, and ideas, while rejecting its most important truths.

Islam makes itself attractive to potential converts in part because it associates temporal and eternal blessing with material pleasures. The Quran speaks of this extensively, promising an eternal abundance of wine, women, and luxury. St. Juan de Ribera noted:

> (Muhammad) paints a picture of heaven as being filled with sensual and fleshly delights. These include orchards, trees, upholsteries, tables, delicacies, and the company of women. All of this does not measure up to the good nature of a thing so noble as man, but is to repugnate his nobility and that of heaven, for heaven being as it is, it cannot contain such brutal and dirty things that you allege.[64]

Another threatening facet of Islamic theology is its endorsement of aggression and violence against unbelievers. This is most commonly associated with jihad, but it includes the oppression of non-Muslims under Islamic law.[65] Under sharia, non-Muslims are allocated to second-class citizenship whereby their existence is conditional upon their accepting a pact of laws particular to them, called a *dhimma*. These people, now called *dhimmis*, or "people of the pact," are allowed to continue to exist within Islamic society a) as long as they follow all provisions and b) as long as the Muslim ruler in power permits their existence. Christians in dhimmitude may be permitted to worship, but not to live and spread their religion with full freedom.

The Church and Islam have always been at opposition to each other, and always will be because their theologies are irreconcilable. Historically they have been unable to peaceably co-exist together in society; inevitably, one has overtaken the other. This was the case in northern Africa, the Middle East, Turkey, Bosnia, and Albania, where Christian populations gave way to Muslim dominance, and in Portugal, Spain, France, Poland, Sicily, Hungary, and Austria, all of which either liberated themselves from Muslim rule or successfully fought off repeated attempts at invasion by Islamic armies. And it's the case today in every part of the world where Muslim populations of any significance co-inhabit lands with Christians or members of other religions. In Europe, which is historically Christian but in recent decades has experienced large waves of Muslim immigration and flat-lining Christian birth rates, nearly all the major cities and many smaller cities now have sizeable Muslim populations. In many of these cities are predominantly

Muslim areas noted for violence against Christians and Jews, and local attempts to enforce sharia.

Chapter 33 of the Quran is entitled *Rome* (*Rum*), and it speaks about the conquest of Rome. Although "Rome" has been explained as standing for Constantinople, since that city was called the Rome of the East by the Byzantines (and conquered by Muslim Turks in 1453), not a few Muslims today understand it to refer to Rome, Italy. (Indeed, in 2015, Muslim terrorists from Syria and Iraq announced, "We will conquer Rome, by Allah's permission."[66]) The conquest of Rome would signify for Islam the conquest and destruction of the Catholic Faith and ultimately, all Christianity.

19. How do you respond to people who claim that it's not tolerant, charitable, or even "Christian" to criticize Islam?

There is a growing fear among people in the West that it's wrong to assert something if it contradicts or gives offense to other beliefs. For Catholics, nothing could be further from the truth. We must be merciful, of course, and make all our criticisms with love and due temperance. However, mercy is conditional upon justice—it is unjust and thus immoral to deny or ignore the grave untruths in Islam, especially as Christ calls us to be a witness to the Faith "in season and out of season" (2 Tim. 4:2).

Either Muhammad is a true prophet or he is a false prophet. Either the Quran's teaching about Jesus is true or it's false. If you believe that Jesus is God, you testify that Muhammad is a false prophet and the Quran's teachings about him are lies. If you say that Muhammad is a true prophet, then Jesus is not God and the gospel is a lie. Naturally, acknowledging this dilemma and taking a strong position in favor of the Faith, even when it is done in kindness, will provoke negative and sometimes aggressive reactions. How should we deal with them?

Outside of Muslims, the biggest defenders of Islam tend to be people who associate criticism of Islam with racism, classism, or political oppression. It is best not to engage such people from a political or secular angle, but from a religious one—let them understand that your disagreements are based on your own faith (which you can invite them to learn more about later).

Then there are those people who see Islam's problems not as something rooted in Islamic theology, but as the fault of a few bad Muslims who pervert their religion's teachings. If you don't have a good working knowledge of what Islam actually teaches (and sometimes even if you do) it can be difficult to communicate with them—so ingrained in Western culture is the notion that Islam is fundamentally a "religion of peace."

In my experience speaking with Muslims who claim it's uncharitable to criticize their religion, I have found no way to demonstrate that one is suitably tolerant toward Islam other than by converting to Islam. Nothing you promise, say, or do will ever be sufficient. This means you have two choices. The first is to remain silent and passive or attempt to explain away differences and problems. However, this can be interpreted as consent to Islamic teachings, and will simply encourage Muslims to press for acceptance of more Islamic teachings with greater aggression. The other option is to speak the truth boldly and unceasingly.

Anybody who says that you must refrain from speaking about your own faith, or from criticizing Islam, for the sake of "tolerance" is wrong and perhaps malicious. For the salvation of souls and in fulfillment of our baptismal vows, we must not censor ourselves, lest we bring condemnation upon ourselves.

20. What's the right way for Catholics to dialogue with Muslims?

Christ commands all Catholics to be witnesses[67] to the world, and so we are required to witness to Muslims as we are required to witness to all people. Each of us must first be a *living witness* by knowing the Faith and living it daily. For most Catholics, this will be all of the witness they will need to give to Muslims. Indeed, *no Catholic is obligated to initiate a religious discussion or debate with a Muslim for any reason.*

But there may be circumstances where you believe a more direct form of witness is called for. This kind of witness must be accompanied by prayer and discernment. You must clearly understand what your goals are, and what you are able and unable to do. You must also be mindful of your personal disposition, since you will be presenting the Faith to people who may be openly hostile to it—and to you.

Based on my experience, when you engage Muslims in religious dialogue it helps to follow certain guidelines:

1. Focus on ideas, not events.

For every example of historical Islamic violence or deviancy you raise, a Muslim will try to throw back two or more in your direction about Christianity, even if those examples are lies or half-truths. This creates a "he said, she said" conversation that ultimately goes nowhere. Instead, focus on the underlying beliefs that drive the actions, because once you establish that an *idea* is accepted by Islam, you can connect it to the actions it bears.

For instance, if you argue that Islam is violent because of the September 11 terrorist attacks, a Muslim may immediately start talking about the Crusades, "Western imperialism," or some other Christian sin real or imagined. This conversation would be destined for failure. Instead, you should ask if Islam *permits* perpetual violence against non-Muslims. Now, even though a Muslim might try to divert the conversation by adding extraneous topics or examples (see rule 2 below), it's still much easier to discuss with him what Islam considers to be divinely revealed truths. Such an approach has the potential to be a good conversation.

2. Keep the conversation to one topic only—no exceptions.

In my experience conversing and arguing with Muslims, I have frequently noted the tactic on their part of raising multiple topics in one or two sentences, and then trying to intimidate me into giving coherent answers on all of them at once, which is impossible. If someone tries to do this, tell him that while you appreciate the questions, you can only focus on one item at a time, and you can discuss the others in a separate conversation later. If he does not respect this, you might as well end the conversation, because he's not actually interested in dialogue.

3. Speak only to what you know definitively.

There is a lot to know about Christianity, and equally so with Islam. If you want to cite specific examples, do so only if you firmly know the sources in question and are able to tie them into your arguments. This pertains to Christian as well as Islamic sources. Remember that even if the Muslim you are speaking with is generally trustful (and trustworthy), there is still a part of his beliefs telling him to distrust and question everything you say.[68]

I have found that when a Muslim asks a question or brings up a matter that you don't know well, the best response is to say, "I don't know," and not engage it. If you are comfortable and able to do so, you may offer to find the answer for him for a future conversation. Doing this not only presents you as an honest person, but as somebody who genuinely cares and is interested in a real conversation. Remember, though: one topic at a time!

4. Critique Islam only from Islamic sources.

Muslims can be the most difficult people to argue religion with, because Islam teaches that criticism of Islam is not only unacceptable, but punishable by death, following the example of Muhammad.[69] Not all Muslims believe this, but oftentimes you will still encounter a defense mechanism as soon as you say anything mildly critical of Islam. This is particularly true when your critique is based on non-Islamic sources. The Muslim may attempt to shut down the conversation, using dishonest arguments or even threats to silence you. So even though it can be useful for your own study to learn what saints, popes, and secular historians have said about Islam, when conversing with Muslims you should avoid referring to them.

If you want to become knowledgeable about what Islamic sources have to say, focus first on a few major subjects. I usually focus on Muhammad's treatment of apostates from Islam, the permissibility of lying to further the cause of Islam, and the permissibility of perpetual aggressive violence against non-Muslims. These are easy points to keep focus on and speak directly to major issues facing Christianity and Islam today.

Even so, I have had Muslims look me in the face and say with complete confidence that I was speaking falsely about Islam even while I had the evidence from their own sacred scripture, tradition, and commentators in my favor, not to mention the support of other Muslims. You will find that Muslims who are accustomed to performing *taqiyya* are able to lie fluently about their own religion. It is a sobering and sometimes aggravating reality, but it is a fact of life when working with Islam.

5. Keep men with men and women with women—never mix the two.

Finally, a small but important piece of advice: if you are a woman who wants to witness to Muslims, you will be more effective if you confine yourself to dealing only with Muslim women. If you're a man, you may find that your only opportunities for dialogue are with other men, since Muslim women are often discouraged from social intercourse with non-Muslim men.

In all cases, remember that criticism of Islam is not an end unto itself, but a vehicle for communicating the truth. So the focus must never be merely on winning arguments. Neither should we make "dialogue" an end in itself; rather it should always be at the service of evangelization. Muslims must see Christ in us, and we must strive to speak to them on Christ's behalf so they he may draw them to himself.

Recommended Reading

There are many excellent books available about Islam. However, nothing can replace reading from the foundational works that define the religion. The following list is not exhaustive, but it's an excellent start if you want to learn more.

The Life of Muhammad (Ibn Ishaq)

Written by the early Muslim writer Ibn Ishaq, translated by Alfred Guillaume, and published continually by Oxford University Press since 1960. If you can only purchase one book about Islam, outside of the Quran, this is it. This book is the oldest biography of Muhammad and is replete with full details of Muhammad's life and deeds.

Sahih Al-Bukhari (Imam Bukhari)

This is the collection of Islamic sacred tradition, or hadith, of Imam Bukhari. His work is considered one of the most reliably collections of Islamic sacred tradition. There are several translations, but I prefer the parallel English-Arabic text translated by Muhammad Muhsin Khan and published by Darussalam Publishers.

Sahih Al-Muslim (Imam Muslim)

This is similar to Bukhari's collection but was compiled at the same time by Imam Muslim. It is a smaller but no less respectable work. There are several translations, but I use the English translation from Abdul Hamid Siddiqi and published by Sheik Muhammad Ashraf Publications of Lahore, Pakistan.

Reliance of the Traveler (Ahmad Ibn Naqib Al-Masry)

If you are interested in Islamic law, Ahmad ibn Naqib Al-Masri's fourteenth-century book translated into English by Nuh Ha Mim Keller is an excellent source. It is simply a law text and so is not particularly engaging, but it is a solid overview and insight into Islamic Sharia law in theory and practice.

Seeing Islam as Others Saw It: A Survey and Evaluation of Christian, Jewish and Zoroastrian Writings on Early Islam (Studies in Late Antiquity and Early Islam) (Robert G. Hoyland)

This brilliantly compiled collection of accounts of the rise of Islam is the only non-Muslim book I recommend here. It contains a wealth of primary source documents that detail the experiences of those conquered by Muslims. I have never found another book like it.

About the Author

Andrew Bieszad has a master's degree in Islamic Studies and Christian-Muslim relations from Hartford Seminary. He is also the author of *Lions of the Faith: Saints, Blesseds, and Heroes of the Catholic Faith in the Struggle with Islam.*

Endnotes

1 Some Muslims say that Islam means "peace." This is incorrect. Because the Arabic language, like Hebrew, has no vowels, all words are based off of three-consonant "roots." Arabic then creates further new words and ideas by adding specific consonant prefixes or suffix patterns. It is accurate to say that the word Islam is *related* to the word peace, which is *salam*. However, the particular grammar pattern used here, called "Form IV" by grammarians, indicates the action in question is forced upon somebody or something. Hence, *Islam* literally means "forced" or "imposed" peace on somebody or something, and hence, *submission*.

2 St. John of Damascus (d. 749), who lived and worked under the Umayyad caliphate in Syria, writes that the stone, called the "black rock" (*Al-Hajar Al-Aswad*), was originally a head from a statue of Aphrodite.

3 The Shia, members of the largest minority Muslim sect, use *imam* to refer to the head of the entire Muslim community, whom they believe receives direct guidance from Allah. Their local clergy in mosques are usually called *mullahs*—although with these terms in Islam there is considerable fluidity and overlap.

4 Bukhari 1:3, and Muslim 1:301 among other places.

5 Quran 96:1–5.

6 The charges listed here against Muhammad are indeed numerous and heinous, but well-grounded in Islam's own literature. Consult the Quran and the hadith collections listed in the appendix for more information about them.

7   Genie, or *jinn*, is synonymous with demons, as the word for
    possessed in Arabic is *majnun*, or "having a genie."

8   Bukhari 47:786 and 53:394 among other places.

9   The hadith are organized into collections, which then are broken
    up into short books. Each story in these books is assigned a
    number. When referencing hadith, they are cited as "Collection
    author Book Number: Story Number." Thus Bukhari's collection,
    book 1, story 2, would be written as "Bukhari 1:2."

10 There have been many good Christian writings about this. For
    an interesting Jewish perspective, see Rabbi Abraham Geiger's
    Judaism and Islam (Originally published 1896. Reprinted by
    Forgotten Books, 2012). In addition, Professor Alan Dundes's
    Fables of the Ancients? (Rowman and Littlefield, 2003) is a
    likewise good place to begin.

11 John 1:1–14.

12 This "eternal Quran" as Allah's uncreated and eternal word is
    called the *Furqan* because it distinguishes (*yatafarraqa*) between
    truth and falsehood. Every paper Quran is a reflection of the
    eternal *Furqan*. Chapter 25 of the Quran is dedicated to the *Furqan*.

13 Ibn Ishaq, *The Life of Muhammad* (New York: Oxford University
    Press, 2002), 165–166.

14 Quran 53:19–20.

15 Quran 22:52.

16 For example, Quran 3:28 permits Muslims to make false
    allegiances with non-Muslims as a "precaution." Ibn Kathir, a
    renowned classical Islamic commentator, adds this: "Should
    one fear in some nation or time some evil of them, then he may
    dissimulate unto them in secret, not in his heart or intention."

He also adds, quoting Ibn Abbas from the same commentary, "Dissimulation is not by action, but with the tongue."

17 Quran 9:5, for instance, which allows Muslims to fight and kill non-Muslims in perpetuity until they convert, abrogates the (chronologically) earlier 109:6, which tolerantly offers, "To you be your way, and to me mine."

18 Quran 2:106.

19 Quran 14:27.

20 See *Lumen Gentium* 16.

21 Quran 3:42, 19:31. Bukhari 54:506, 55:641, 60:71. Muslim 30:5837, 30:5838. The understanding is that Satan touches all children when they are born, and the only ones which he did not touch were Jesus and Mary.

22 Quran 5:46, 57:27. Islam teaches that the Gospels contained originally what is in the Quran, but they were corrupted by the apostles and early Christians.

23 Quran 4:157–158.

24 Quran 2:140, 3:78 among other places.

25 Perhaps not coincidentally, the town of Fatima, Portugal was the site of the twentieth century's greatest Marian apparition, in 1917.

26 Fulton J. Sheen, *The World's First Love* (New York: McGraw-Hill Book Company, 1952), 208.

27 "Narrated Abu Huraira: The prophet said, "Every child is born with a true faith of Islam and his parents convert him to Judaism or Christianity or Magianism." Bukhari 23:467.

28 Quran 95:4–6.

29 Quran 2:65. This is referring to a group of Jews that Allah turned into swine and pigs.

30 Bukhari 84:57.

31 Dhimmi laws have been in place since the inception of Islam. In the past, these laws took the form of a literal written pact which was usually signed by a leader representing the Christians of an area. In modern times, they have been enshrined in the common laws of Islamic societies. Contemporary examples include Iran, Pakistan, and Saudi Arabia, which permit Christians to enter and live within their borders, but under harsh restrictions with even graver penalties for violations.

32 From *Forty Hadith* by Imam Nawawi, hadith #32. The understanding here is that as far as non-Muslims are concerned, it is of no consequence how one relates to them so long as one does not act in a way that is clearly detrimental to the interest of Islam or Muslims, and this is obviously subject to interpretation. This is not a prohibition against doing them harm or a command to do right, but simply a decree of neutrality permitting both states.

33 Perhaps the Spanish situation best illustrates this. Many times Spain had come close to expelling the occupying Muslims, but Muslims from what is today Morocco rallied together under the banner of Islam and launched invasions that quickly destroyed the Spanish Catholics' gains. This happened most notably in 1084 with the Almoravids and in 1146 with the Almohads, and the armies dissipated into their own factions almost as fast as they had formed.

34 Matt. 26:52.

35 Bukhari 2:24.

36 See Muslim 1:31.

37 Story related in 2 Kings 25. Jeremiah and Isaiah also both spoke

extensively about Israel's sins and her coming destruction on account of her refusal to repent.

38 Quran 9:29.

39 Quran 4:89.

40 Quran 5:33.

41 Quran 8:65.

42 Quran 47:4.

43 Quran 66:9.

44 The Crusades to the Holy Land are the best known today, but there were other Crusades that took place within Europe; for example, the Albigensian Crusade in southern France from 1209–1229.

45 Taken from Ibn Jubayr, *The Travels of Ibn Jubayr*, trans. Ronald Broadhurst, (London: J. Cape, 1952), 315.

46 *Nostra Aetate* 3.

47 Gen. 16:12.

48 Gen. 22:17.

49 John 4:22.

50 Quran 2:125.

51 Quran 3:3, 7:157, 35:31. None of these Quranic passages actually say that the Bible or Torah was corrupted. To the contrary, they say that the Quran confirms the messages of these books. Muslims make the assumption that because the Bible and Torah do not match the Quran's words, then Christians and Jews must have corrupted their texts.

52 Bukhari 92:461.

53 See Heb. 10:16.

54 See Matt. 11:28–30.

55 Islam is fairly silent on the issue of abortion, and sources are scarce and difficult to acquire, even in Arabic. The Quranic commentators are silent, and most of the debates come from the first centuries of Islam from the four "schools" of though (Hanafi, Maliki, Shafi, and Hanbali, in order of progressively more conservative). There is universal agreement that after 120 days, abortion is a sin. Imam Shafi makes the most pronounced statements in his *Fiqh*. This reasoning is based on the hadith from Bukhari 54:430 and 93:546.

56 See Robert Spencer, *Not Peace but a Sword* (San Diego: Catholic Answers Press, 2013), 16–18.

57 Quran 4:15, 24:2–4. See also Bukhari 63:196, 82:806, 82:810, 82:814 and Muslim 17:4198, 17:4199. The hadith examples do not pertain to women, but emphasize that four witnesses or a confession made four times suffices under Islamic law for conviction, and these hadith are cited by Islam as evidence for this.

58 Quran 4:3, 33:50.

59 Quran 4:3. Although this same passage permits marriage up to four women, it notes that Muslims may take any number of women ("what your right hand possesses") as spoils of war.

60 Quran 3:28.

61 Quran 5:51.

62 For more historical detail see my book, *Lions of the Faith: Saints, Blesseds, and Heroes of the Catholic Faith in the Struggle with Islam*. Lux Orbis Press, 2013.

63 Ibn Khaldun, *The Muqaddimah: An Introduction to History*, trans. Franz Rosenthal (Princeton, NJ: Princeton University Press, 2005), 188.

64 St. Juan de Ribera. *Catechismo para la Instruccion de los Nuevos Convertidos de los Moros* (1599).

65 See Quran 9:29.

66 ISIS video release. February 15th, 2015.

67 See Matt. 28:19, Acts 1:8.

68 Quran 5:51.

69 Quran 83:13–17. See also Ishaq 149–150, 363–369, 550, 597–602, 675–676 for an extensive list of persons assassinated by Muhammad for criticizing Islam. Many of these were pagan poets who were executed for mocking Islam or Muhammad's carnal lust.

Become part of the team.
Help support Catholic Answers.

Catholic Answers is an apostolate dedicated to serving Christ by bringing the fullness of Catholic truth to the world. We help good Catholics become better Catholics, bring former Catholics "home," and lead non-Catholics into the fullness of the Faith.

Catholic Answers neither asks for nor receives financial support from any diocese. The majority of its annual income is in the form of donations from individual supporters like you.

To make a donation by phone using your credit card, please speak with one of our customer service representatives at 888-291-8000.

To make a donation by check, please send a check payable to "Catholic Answers" to:

> Catholic Answers
> 2020 Gillespie Way
> El Cajon, CA 92020

To make a donation online, visit **catholic.com**.

TO EXPLAIN & DEFEND THE FAITH

catholic.com